HAVANT

❧ *The Golden Years* ❧

PETER ROGERS AND STEVE JONES

HALSGROVE

First published in Great Britain in 2002

British Library Cataloguing-in-Publication Data
A CIP record for this title is available from the British Library

ISBN 1 84114 182 8

HALSGROVE

Halsgrove House
Lower Moor Way
Tiverton, Devon EX16 6SS
Tel: 01884 243242
Fax: 01884 243325
email: sales@halsgrove.com
website: www.halsgrove.com

Printed and bound in Great Britain by Bookcraft (Bath) Ltd, Midsomer Norton

❧ CONTENTS ❧

PREFACE

In 1952 following the death of King George VI, the accession to the throne of HM Queen Elizabeth II was accompanied by constitutional reform. She was proclaimed in each of the self-governing countries of what used to be called the British Empire, as Queen of that particular country. The formal abandonment of the indivisibility of the Crown was confirmed by statute in 1953 and a new description, Head of the Commonwealth, was inserted among the royal titles to allow for the inclusion of republics such as India and Pakistan. A feature of the reign has been the number of independent states that have since come into being.

Parallels, though seemingly unimportant, may be drawn with our own national and local forms of government; the removal and subsequent loss, of several traditional county names, together with boundary changes (including those of our own home County of Hampshire), the upgrading of towns to city status and, in 1974, Havant incorporated as a borough.

Allowing that multiple and important changes have affected us all in one way or another in the intervening years, 1952 has also been chosen as the year in which to commence this pictorial compilation. It depicts fifty years of change in the growth and development of the Borough of Havant, and acknowledges and celebrates, together with Her Majesty, fifty golden years.

INTRODUCTION

In geographical terms the boundaries of Havant have changed little during the transition and change of administration titles; from Havant Rural District Council in 1894, to Havant and Waterloo Urban District Council in 1932, and to Havant Borough Council in 1974.

During this period however, population figures have increased from 10,000 in 1900 to 20,000 in 1946, and to 115,000 at the achievement of borough status in 1974.

This population explosion has been due, in no small measure, to the creation of the Leigh Park council housing estate and, with it, an influx of many families who had lost their homes in the Portsmouth air raids of the Second World War. (It is recorded that multiple raids on the city had destroyed or damaged 80,000 properties.)

In 1920 and again in 1932, Portsmouth had extended its boundaries from the limited confines of Portsea Island to include mainland Cosham, Drayton and Farlington.

In 1949 following the end of the war, land-hungry Portsmouth sought to establish a 'satellite' town, this time within the administrative area of Havant and Waterloo UDC. An astute purchase of Leigh Park House and grounds in 1943, 1671 acres at a price of £80 per acre, followed by a later purchase of an additional 198 acres, had given Portsmouth a total of 2469 acres on which to create a virtual 'new town' which was later to become the largest council housing estate in Great Britain.

Development continued apace from 1950 until 1966 when the last of the Portsmouth council housing was completed at West Leigh, Wakefords and Sharpes Copse.

Opinions were divided as to whether or not this 'new town' located within Havant was an agreeable addition or, as was sometimes suggested, 'a cuckoo in the nest'!

In the early years, most of the immigrant working population returned daily to Portsmouth where their traditional sources of employment were still to be found; few of them having the luxury of motor transport, many made the 20-mile round trip by bicycle or bus.

In contrast to Portsmouth, Havant's traditional industries such as parchment-making, tanning, milling, brewing and the production of watercress, had come to an end or were ceasing production. Changes were to take place, however, when, attracted by a ready source of local labour and the willingness of Havant planners to allocate suitable building sites, a number of major manufacturers made the decision to relocate to the area; industrial estates being established at New Lane, Brockhampton and Broadmarsh in addition to those in Leigh Park itself. High-tech companies of international standing were to become familiar names in Havant e.g., Wyeth, Vickers-Sperry, Avery Hardoll Kenwood, IBM, Colt International, Minimodels (Scalextric) etc.

To cater for a rapidly increasing population, schools, colleges, health centres, police headquarters, libraries, shopping centres etc. were built to supplement those already existing.

It is to be remembered of course, that whilst the town of Havant was experiencing a post-war boom in new development and prosperity, then so were the other districts within the borough: Waterlooville, Purbrook, Cowplain, Emsworth and Hayling Island. Each of them growing in size, population, prosperity and popularity, they are, together with 'Mother Hen' Havant, part of the 'so called' affluent South.

This book will portray through its many illustrations, the changes that have taken place in each district within the Borough of Havant, changes which may have affected each of us in our daily lives.

Topographical scenes will remind us of occasional chaotic traffic problems experienced before the construction of the A27 bypass and the A3M motorway around both Havant and Waterlooville.

Local personalities from the past will be recalled as old, familiar faces and events are revealed. It will be considered inconceivable by many readers that incidents within the last fifty years have slipped entirely from memory whilst other happenings remain within total recall. The younger generation of readers may well be astonished to know that there was a time when the motor car did not reign supreme, that Havant, Waterlooville and Hayling Island each had a cinema and that it had been possible to travel to Hayling by train.

Allowing that the years 1952 to 2002 have witnessed great and sometimes near impossible changes within the borough, the natural environment of the area remains much as it has always been; Emsworth, Havant, Bedhampton and Hayling each having a share of the south Hampshire coastline whilst the closeness of the surrounding countryside affords almost immediate access to the delights of the Hampshire and West Sussex Downlands with their unique and unspoilt villages.

Together with these natural amenities, a modern road and motorway system, along with adequate rail and ferry services, continue to provide the traveller with a ready route to and from London, Portsmouth, Brighton, Southampton, the Isle of Wight and other centres.

Over the fifty years, a harmonious blend of old and new has been maintained. The borough has increased in size, stature and prosperity, remaining, as it always has been, an attractive and agreeable place in which to live and work.

The proof is within these pages that we have no need to travel back to pre-history to study the past … read on, wallow in a little nostalgia, relive old memories, make comparisons and marvel at the present age in which we live.

ACKNOWLEDGEMENTS

Whilst the compilation and editing of *Havant – The Golden Years* has been the responsibility of Peter Rogers and Steve Jones, the task of gathering and compiling illustrations and information for this book has been made all the more pleasant by the willing response and assistance of many people without whose help, advice and expertise, the publication would not have been possible. No one person or institution can therefore claim credit for its ultimate success.

We have to express our thanks to: The Curator, Dr Christopher Palmer, and colleagues at Havant Museum, together with members of the Society of Friends of Havant Museum, Hampshire County Museums Service, members of Havant Borough Council's Planning Department and Portsmouth City Museums and Records Office.

Individual contributors include Councillor Ralph Cousins, Russell Fox, Ilse McKee, Joan Swatton, Arthur Ricketts, Tessa Daines, Malcolm Smith, Audrey Rogers, Gavin Maidment, David Jordan, Anthony Triggs, John Pile, Peter Barge, Julia Goddard, Steve Barber, Richard Fowler, David Oliver, David Welch, Susan Sherwood, Eric Udal, Stuart Hales, Adrian Gardiner, Peter Williams, Betty Marshall, Christine Housely, Anne Griffiths, Anne Welsted, Andrew Perrin, David Bolt, Phil Hammond, Noel Pycroft, Doug McKenzie, the Seacourt Tennis Club and the Avenue Lawn Tennis Club.

We are particularly grateful to the generosity of photographers Michael Edwards and Alan Bell for allowing the use of original photographs, which constitute perhaps one-third of all the illustrations.

A number of aerial views in this compilation are credited to C.J. Brunnen of Cosham whose co-operation is much appreciated.

C J Brunnen Photography
S. E. B. Building
Medina Road
Cosham
Portsmouth PO6 3NH
023 9232 4591
www.cjbphotography.co.uk

As most, if not all of the illustrations are from accredited sources, any infringement of copyright seems unlikely but we do ask forgiveness should there be any transgression.

With the exception of material taken from the Havant and Hampshire County Museums collections and those professional photographers already named, an easy reference to the contributors of additional illustrations is given below:

P.B.	Peter Barge	I.M.	Ilse McKee
A.B.	Alan Bell	D.M.	Doug. McKenzie
S.B.	Steve Barber	A.P.	Andrew Perrin
R.C.	Ralph Cousins	J.P.	John Pile
T.D.	Tessa Daines	N.P.	Noel Pycroft
M.E.	Michael Edwards	A.R.	Arthur Ricketts
R.F.	Russell Fox	S.S.	Sue Sherwood, Avenue L.T.C.
A.G.	Adrian Gardiner	J.S.	Joan Swatton
S.H.	Stuart Hales	A.T.	Anthony Triggs
H.B.C.	Havant Borough Council	E.U.	Eric Udal, Avenue L.T.C.
D.J.	David Jordan	D.W.	David Welch
P.W.	Peter Williams		

The combined resources of so many individuals and organisations will hopefully produce a pictorial record worthy of its title, 'The Golden Years'.

The Friends of Havant Museum (a registered charity) will be the sole beneficiaries of revenue generated from the sale of this book.

Our SUNDAY Programmes

AUGUST 2nd
MADELEINE CARROLL - STERLING HAYDEN
BAHAMA PASSAGE
TECHNICOLOR (U)

RICHARD DENNING - DISASTER (A)

AUGUST 9th
BURT LANCASTER - BARBARA STANWYCK
SORRY, WRONG NUMBER (A)

HOOT GIBSON - FEUD OF THE WEST (U)

AUGUST 16th
BOB HOPE
LOUISIANA PURCHASE
Technicolor

AUGUST 23rd
DONALD O'CONNOR - PATRICIA MEDI
FRANCIS (U)

THE RANGE BUSTERS - KID'S LAST RIDE (U)

AUGUST 30th
RANDOLPH SCOTT - BARBARA BRIT
ABILENE TOWN (A)

WILLIAM TR

Forthcoming Attractions

Jack Hawkins
The Cruel Sea (U)

—

Budd Abbott - Lou Costello
Abbott & Costello meet Captain Kidd
CINECOLOR (U)

—

Alastair Sim - Ronald Shiner
Claire Bloom - Margaret Rutherford
Innocents in Paris (A)

Don Taylor
(A)

Empire Havant
PHONE 179

CONTINUOUS
DAILY from 5 p.m.
Doors open 4.45 p.m.
Wed., Sat. and Bank Holidays
from 2.15 p.m.
Doors open 2 p.m.
SUNDAYS from 5—10 p.m.
Doors open 4.45 p.m.

Attractions for
 AUGUST

PRICES Incl. Tax
1/- 1/9 2/3 2/8
Reduced prices for Children when
accompanied by their parents
LARGE FREE CAR PARK

★ A SHIPMAN & KING THEATRE

CHAPTER ONE
❧ HAVANT TOWN ☙

West Street 1934. This early photograph is included so that comparisons
may be made when viewing the same street in the several pictures appear-
ing in this book covering the last fifty years. Older readers may recall the
businesses trading here which, with the exception of Davies the Chemist,
have all disappeared. The Dolphin Hotel, referred to elsewhere in this
volume, is seen in its setting of sixty-eight years ago. Across the road, the
two bicycles beneath the 'Gold Flake' advertisement, are standing exactly on
the spot where, in 1977, a Roman second-century well was discovered; coin-
cidentally, perhaps, at the corner of the small street named The Homewell!

A.T.

This stunning aerial photograph of 1999 shows that St Faith's Church still dominates the town centre amid all the many changes of the past fifty years. The Meridian Centre occupies a large part of the town to the north of the church.

C.J.B.

The Dolphin Hotel, West Street, Havant was demolished to make way for the West Street pedestrian arcade c.1958. This same location now provides entrance into the Meridian Centre. In 1830, the hotel was described as the 'Principal Inn of Havant' and 'a convenient and well accustomed house'. The rear of the building once boasted a bowling green. A corn market was formerly held on Saturdays during the nineteenth century. It was also a 'post house' bringing mail from both Southampton and Brighton. In 1903, along with several Havant Inns, it was purchased by the Horndean Brewery of George Gale & Co. A new Dolphin public house in Park Road South has since replaced the original.

M.E.

Photographed during the Queen's Silver Jubilee year of 1977, the Pelham Bookshop, West Street, was always a popular venue for Havant bibliophiles. Originally built in 1798, probably as a flour and corn merchants, the shop has had a varied history. At one time it belonged to the well-known Havant firm of Fay, Plumbers & Decorators; now, however, this eye-catching building is popular for its variety of lunch-time pastries and snacks in the pavement café setting of La Bonne Baguette.

This 1966 photograph is of Dittman & Malpas, West Street. Older readers will recall branches of this corn and seed merchant in each of our local towns. The Havant store, whilst still trading under its original name, is now a mecca for those wishing to purchase fine glass and chinaware.

M.E.

Another view of West Street in 1958, showing the north side of the road looking towards what is now the entrance to the Meridian Centre. Almost all the buildings photographed were later demolished and replaced with a modern shopping centre.

M.E

Traffic passes through a busy West Street in the 1970s prior to the road being pedestrianised.

With a police officer keeping an eye on proceedings, members of a Havant Scout group lead a Youth Parade through the streets towards St Faith's Church in June 1962.

M.E.

Looking much the worse for wear on a wet day in March 1958, West Street is pictured before the much needed redevelopment of the town centre. The buildings opposite and to the right of Pelham Library were all later demolished and replaced with modern shops.

M.E.

West Street 1987. Completed by July 1983, pedestrianisation made it safe for shoppers to walk without fear of traffic. The precinct is now home to a popular twice-weekly market.

Shoppers in Havant were intro- duced to off-street shopping when, after the removal of the Dolphin Hotel in 1958, the West Street Arcade was opened for business. With no 'big-name' stores involved, customers had probably a greater choice of goods in the small, individual businesses than in the well-known High Street stores which now dominate town-centre shopping nationwide. All too soon, it seems, the arcade was demol- ished in favour of the present Meridian Shopping Centre.

R.C.

Passing the Cobden Arms in West Street, the decorated floats carry members of the Young Conservatives' Association who are rallying to express their grievances against the Government in the early 1960s.

M.E.

The ultimate in modern motoring fashion in the 1960s, Haulgo advertises scooters and 'bubble' cars on the pavement outside its showroom at the corner of West Street and Brockhampton Lane. Though no longer dealing in 'speedy' transport, the site is today that of the Speedy Hire-Tool Centre.

M.E.

Smiling council employees display their own 'latest model' machine, a new dustcart, in West Street, September 1961. The building behind them, by this date derelict, had been the premises of Cuff's Shoe Repairs. Later to be demolished, the site became part of Henry Jones, Builders.

M.E.

Displayed in the May sunshine of 1959, smart prams and pushchairs are the latest mode of transport for Havant's junior population. Eric Keast, Smeed & Smeed wine merchants, J.B. Cusworth newsagents and W. Wadsworth pharmacist, were all later replaced with a modern parade of shops.

M.E.

Michael Edwards, photographer and 'part-time' adventurer, involved himself in every facet of the Havant scene from around 1953 until his retirement in 1987. Recording marriages, day-to-day events and many changes within the town, as well as providing studio facilities, he also found time for his adventures. These have included touring worldwide in his veteran car and a cycle tour of Europe and Asia. In retirement, he is still a keen cyclist and an active member of a local cycle club. We are grateful for his generosity in allowing access to so many photographs from his archive.

M.E

Whoops! This accident occurred at a location unrecognisable today, the junction of West Street with Park Road North. Civic Offices, the large brick building, have been replaced by the Parchment Makers, a Wetherspoon public house.

M.E.

A fine building that is now lost to Bedhampton was the Froebel House School. Previously known as Brocklands, the school was run along lines drawn up by German educationist Friedrich Froebel whose aim was to 'help the child's mind grow naturally and spontaneously'. The premises had earlier been the residence of Admiral Stephen Poyntz until purchased by Frank Stent, a member of the well-known Havant family.

M.E.

With a history more in keeping with a courtroom than a public house it is not surprising that this listed building changed its name from the Black Dog to the Courthouse in 1996. Throughout most of the nineteenth century the Black Dog in West Street acted as the Magistrates Court, with such local dignitaries as Sir Frederick Fitzwygram of Leigh Park and John Deverell of Purbrook overseeing the Petty Sessions. Before the Town Hall was built, the Black Dog Assembly Rooms were used for important town meetings as well as a place of entertainment for the people of Havant.

M.E

Attending the Remembrance Day Service at St Faith's Church 1954, are Mr Blanch the standard bearer for the Havant British Legion with Mr C.W. Brian, Mr Shoesmith and the Revd Standing, one-time equerry to King George VI.

Remembrance Sunday 1961 and members of the services, youth groups, veterans of two world wars and civic leaders gather to pay their respects at the annual service at the Havant War Memorial.

M.E.

In 1975 it was considered that the tower, or turret, clock was unreliable and should be replaced by a modern and more reliable mechanism. The old clock mechanism, installed when the church was rebuilt in 1860, was rescued by local architect Mr T.K. Makins who stored the parts in his garage. In 1988 he donated the parts to the Hampshire County Museums Service where the clock was restored to working order by conservation staff. The clock can now be seen working in the Havant Museum.

The loss of HMS *Havant* and those of her crew who died at the evacuation of Dunkirk in June 1940 were recalled at a ceremony at St Faith's Church in July 1990 when memorial windows were unveiled. The windows, costing £1500, were paid for by donations, flag days and a contribution by the Royal British Legion whose crest is displayed in the south window; the ship's crest occupying the north window.

In this enhanced photograph, HMS *Havant* occupies the centre window.

The ladies of St Faith's Church choose to stage an alfresco jumble sale on what would appear to be a cold and windy day in 1962.

A happy gathering in 1953 of members of St Faith's Mothers' Union.

With devastating ferocity, the hurricane of October 1987 claimed more than 15 million trees in southern England as well as severely affecting property. Havant and the surrounding districts did not escape unscathed; 700 trees were uprooted at Staunton Country Park and Havant Thicket and damage throughout the borough was immense. In the churchyard of St Faith's, a row of limes crashed down on gravestones but miraculously did little harm to the church.

H.B.C.

Homewell is the name of the short, narrow street which terminates at its southern end as a cul-de-sac. It is also the name given to a natural spring and small pool at the end of the street, a spring which, legend has it, has never failed to produce. This is almost certainly the source from which the townsfolk once obtained their water and its close proximity to the church and centre of the ancient settlement seems to confirm that fact. However, the 1970s discovery of a Roman well a mere 100 yards distant perhaps supports the belief that a contained well was a better source of pure water than an open, easily polluted 'pond'.

H.B.C.

The buildings of the old parchment works form the background to this view of the Homewell pool. Open to the elements and easily contaminated, the pool which should be a source of local pride has been frequently abused. This photograph tells it own tale.

H.B.C.

An answer to the pollution problem was decided upon in the shape of this wall built to contain the pool.

H.B.C.

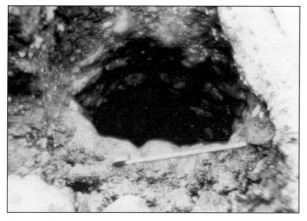

In 1977 this second-century Roman well was discovered at the corner of Homewell and West Street.

Despite exciting considerable interest among local archaeologists, the well was for others little more than a 'nine-days' wonder'. Sited below a public pavement and for safety reasons alone, it is pictured being filled and capped.

SAGA OF THE SPRING

A poem penned by an anonymous 'Disenchanted Old Havantonian' gives a dissenting view of the situation:

Look What They've Done To Our Spring

They've built a wall around our spring,
a 2ft ugly rough old thing,
They say this makes a tourist attraction,
did they have to take such drastic action?

When we were kids our spring was a joy
to every girl and every boy
with a jam-jar from Mum and a net made by Dad,
they were carefree magical times that we had.

They've built a wall around our spring
now today's little kids can't see a thing.
Dogs and birds and horses too
can't drink from the edge like they used to do.

They've built a wall around our spring,
what a sad and useless unkind thing.
If this is enchantment then oh dear me,
I'm glad that I'm sixty and not just three!

Anon.

East Street c.1985 features the same building profiles as of old although almost all of the business names have now changed, Barclays Bank being the only one still recognisable today. Advertised here as for sale, Messrs Ryan the ironmongers for many years occupied the building with a classical façade on the corner of South Street, whilst opposite, on the corner of North Street, the White Hart (the second public house of the name to occupy the site) advertises itself in time-honoured fashion with a traditional, hanging sign. Regrettably, in keeping with many other hostelries, the pub has recently undergone a name change to that of the Malt and Hops. The zebra crossing in the foreground was the first to appear in Havant.

An alternative view of East Street, probably photographed on the same day,
but this time showing the north side of the road.

East Street 1962. Before the provision of the Havant bypass East Street was
the only route through the town. Scenes such as this were happily quite rare
and, with a skilled driver, the narrow thoroughfare could be negotiated. On
this occasion the several bystanders were no doubt giving advice such as,
'Left hand down a bit!'

M.E.

The Gazebo, pictured in December 1961, was built in the late-eighteenth century (the date 1779 is displayed on the weather vane) by William Lellyett in the gardens of what are now 23 and 25 East Street. Made with local brick, it would have originally looked out towards the Manor House and the Fair Field.

In 1982 the Gazebo was on the point of collapse. With the help of donations by local residents and businesses, together with grants from Havant Borough Council, the Monument Trust and the local History Society, the Bosmere Hundred Society organised restoration of the walls and roof. A small garden has since been created based on an eighteenth-century design and using plants representative of the period.

M.E.

Now fully restored, the Gazebo in an intimate, secluded, garden setting, is an oasis from the busy street-life of the town.

Once a favourite haunt of movie fans, the Empire opened in 1936 to replace the old cinema in North Street and finally closed its doors owing to the then general decline in cinema attendance. Following demolition the site was redeveloped as a residential block, retaining a link with the past with its name, Empire Court.

D.J.

This, the first of three photographs of East Street, is c.1943 and helps to illustrate the changes which have since taken place in just one local thoroughfare. The Royal Marine Band is visiting the town during a wartime 'Silver Lining Week', intended to help lift the spirits of the nation. It is also a poignant record of buildings which have long vanished such as: the Empire Cinema; Seward Bros. Motor Engineers (with petrol pumps sited on the pavement!); Gardners Art Store with its original frontage; and Geo. Bentley which then occupied the corner premises.

In 1974 the cinema is still in business. The motor engineers now trade under the name of R.A.Vine (by this time it had become illegal to dispense petrol from pavement pumps). Gardners Art Store has undergone a facelift and, for a while at least, Bentley still occupies the corner site.

H.B.C.

February 2002 and yet more structural changes. The Empire cinema has been replaced by Empire Court and the site of the motor engineers serves an entirely different purpose as the Havant Job Centre.

Now forming part of Havant Arts Centre, the old Town Hall in East Street was constructed in 1870 at a cost of £1500. Designed by Richard Drew, the architect of Leigh Park House, and built with bricks made at Leigh Park, the Town Hall served the people of Havant for more than a century. By 1977, the building was considered to be both outdated and lacking in space and was superceded by new Civic Offices. An imaginative solution was found for the old building when the premises were reopened in 1978 as The Arts Centre.

Members of Havant Town Council attend a meeting in the Council Chamber of the old Town Hall, East Street, September 1957. Before the building of the new Civic Centre, much of the town business was conducted from here. Among those attending are: Messrs Paxton, Nelthorpe, Sparoe, Mrs Perraton and the Town Secretary Mr Forder.

M.E.

Havant Museum first opened to the public on 10 October 1979. Built in 1874 as a home for Miss Mary Charge, the imposing property was originally named Lymbourne because of its close proximity to the stream of that name. The owner, who was of a musical disposition, frequently staged musical evenings in a large purpose-built room. It is believed that a later owner kept up the musical tradition by installing a large pipe organ in the hall. During the Second World War, the house accommodated members of the WRNS who served locally.

Visitors to Havant Museum will be familiar with a tableau depicting a wild-fowler preparing his punt-gun prior to a shooting expedition in Langstone Harbour. Mr Brian Chilvers who had originally used the punt and gun presented them to the museum in 1982. They have been on permanent display since 1990.

In 1988 a much needed gallery extension was completed at the rear of the building to accommodate temporary exhibitions and more ambitious displays of local interest. A paved garden area was also created where occasional outdoor functions could be staged.

Members of the Legio Secunda Augusta, a Roman re-enactment society, entertain visitors to the museum on 10 August 1992.

An event which attracted 'Morris' enthusiasts to the museum in February 2002 was a visit of the popular 'Portsmouth Victory Morris' who attended the retirement of long-serving staff member Ted Heath, himself a member of the group.

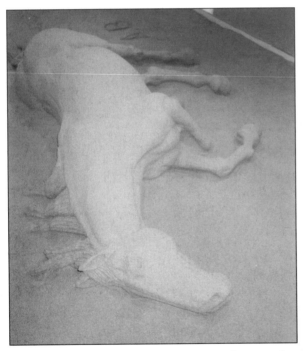

In terms of visitor numbers, the most popular attraction ever exhibited at Havant Museum has been the 'Sand Horse'. Sculpted by Andrew Baynes, the full-size replica horse had pride of place in the exhibition gallery in September/October 1995, during which time 6112 members of the public came to view this incredible sculpture created entirely from three tons of Cornish sand!

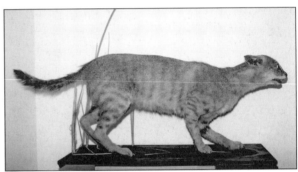

Repeated sightings of a local 'beast' by Hayling Islanders proved to be more solid than just local myth when in 1988 this creature was killed in West Lane after being struck by a car. The animal, identified by zoologists as an African swamp cat, went on display at Havant Museum after being dealt with by a taxidermist. Island folk still insist that there is yet another such creature remaining at large.

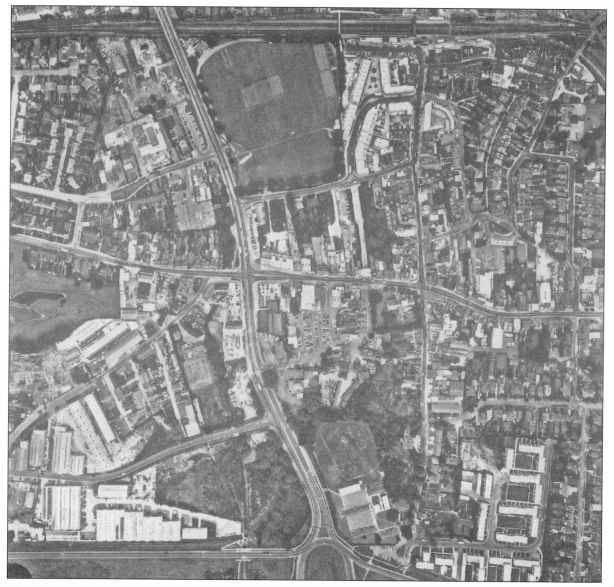

The changing face of Havant is pictured in this view of the town centre in 1970. The new shopping arcades in Market Parade and North Street are seen close to Havant Park while, to the left of the scene, the new bypass which took most of the traffic away from the town centre is clearly shown.

H.B.C.

This unfortunate incident was photographed at the junction of The Pallant and North Street in April 1958. At this time Preston Watson, wine merchants, occupied the building on the left-hand corner where the Waitrose store is now located.

Complementary to the previous photograph, the right-hand turning is The Pallant with the premises of Preston Watson occupying a corner position. The notice 'Acquired for Redwing Properties Ltd' is an indication that the entire block has been selected for redevelopment as the Havant branch of Waitrose Ltd.

The imminent opening of the new Waitrose store in 1979 meant the demolition of almost all of the east side of North Street, and with it the loss of one of the town's oldest businesses, Vines butchers' shop. The occasion was marked by staff who gathered for this photograph on the final day of trading.

M.E.

In a scene from 1982 the North Street approach to the railway station has largely escaped the redevelopment of the past twenty years. The North Street Arcade, however, once the location of the town market, has been the only concession allowed by the planners.

In the only known photograph of the Havant Market, a local troop of Boy
Scouts advertise 'BIG BARGAINS FOR YOU' in a bid to raise funds for their
group in April 1958. The market had closed in 1956, being no longer viable
after several years of decline. The town received its first charter from King
John authorising a weekly market, which was to endure for seven-hundred
years. After several moves, the market site was established here at the top
of North Street at the start of the twentieth century. The location is now that
of the North Street Arcade.

M.E.

Market Way development 1962. No further comment needed here; the progress is self-explanatory.

M.E

Market Way 1963.

M.E.

Popular gentlemen's outfitters Messrs McFall's, since replaced by a ladies' dress shop and a homeopathy clinic, advertises its range of Christmas gifts in December 1961. The building remains one of the few older premises to have escaped the later redevelopment of North Street.

M.E.

Family butcher J.H. Stubbs served Havant folk for more than sixty years but finally succumbed to the planners, together with neighbouring Jessamine House, when the site was cleared to make way for building of the Trustee Savings Bank.

Photographed in 1969, one of the finest 'town' houses in Havant took its name from the white Jessamine that once covered the building. In May 1919 the house was taken over by the Red Cross and became known as the Jessamine Club with the object of 'encouraging members to revive and maintain old friendships forged during the war and to promote good fellowship among the residents of Havant and District'. Now demolished, the site became that of a high street bank which later met the same fate in a continuing programme of redevelopment.

M.E.

Hants 22 V.A.D.

Headquarters

and

Jessamine Club.

President :

MRS. PAXTON.

Hon. Treasurer :

MISS NORAH E. M. LEWIS.

Hon. Secretary :

MISS BRUCE.

ROGERS, PRINTER, HAVANT.

Jessamine Club.

Continuing with business premises removed from the west side of North Street in the replanning process, is the tobacconist, confectioners and café of A.F. & E.F. Blacktopp. Thanks to the 'Beechnut' and 'Y.Z.' chewing gum machines displayed on the wall, it is possible to date the photograph to the 1950s.

Few people would now know that the small house on the left of the photograph was, for many years, the home and office of the Havant Registrar of Births, Deaths and Marriages. Supervised by Miss Best until the 1960s, her appointment followed that of her father who had previously held the office.

In 1989 a weary looking terrace awaits the bulldozers on the west side of North Street.

Havant Library was demolished to make way for the Meridian Shopping Centre, its former site in North Street having acquired a chequered history. Originally built as a single-storey cinema in 1913, it operated as such until 1936. During the war the building was used as an Admiralty torpedo storage depot and in 1950 was purchased by Reeves Builders Merchants who added a first floor and altered the interior. In May 1970 the premises were sold to Hampshire County Council and used as the main Public Library until its closure in 1988.

R.C.

Following the closure of the North Street library and prior to the opening of the new branch in the Meridian Centre, a temporary site was used next to the multi-storey car park. The photograph is dated May 1992.

H.B.C.

This short terrace of Grade Two listed cottages in The Pallant was saved
from demolition by the supermarket chain of Waitrose in the 1970s.

Built in 1728 as a place of worship for Nonconformists, the independent chapel was disposed of in 1890. Now protected under the Town and Country Planning Act of 1972, the building has been used over the years by a variety of commercial concerns, more recently as a wholesale carpet warehouse. Now standing empty it awaits the next episode in a fascinating history.

Prince George Street, January 1962, was once graced with many period houses and cottages. Now they have almost all gone, victims to the overzealous developers of the 1960s and 1970s.

In 1952 personnel of the Havant Fire Brigade, including Station Officer Gillard, pose for the camera at the old Havant Fire Station at Gosslyn House, West Street. In 1955 a new, purpose-built station was opened in Park Way.

In 1963 the brigade is pictured at the later Park Way Headquarters. Unfortunately, after almost forty years, memories have faded regarding why the trophy was awarded to the Havant Brigade; perhaps a past serving member can offer an explanation?

M.E.

In what was reputedly a 'contrived' situation at Oak Park School, Havant, the brigade disposes of, by fire, an old and unsightly wooden store shed.

With the exercise and demonstration over, all that remains now is the clearing-up process.

The march of progress and loss of a walnut tree which had graced the town centre long before the present North and South Park Roads crossed West Street. The site of the tree is now that of Halfords' premises, The Bike Hut. The major building in the view, which served as council offices, has also been demolished and replaced with the Parchment Makers, a Wetherspoon public house.

M.E.

The Brockhampton premises of hairdresser Jess Hunt were, at this time, just beyond the town planners' brief and the inevitable closure order which later would include this quiet backwater of Havant.

M.E.

A wartime measure, originally called British Restaurants, was introduced in many towns to help feed the nation. In some towns it continued for some years afterwards, with a change of title to Civic Restaurant. The picture shows the Nissen hut building in Parkway, still providing the service in 1958.

M.E.

This picture from 1959 reveals a new use for the building when it became Havant Timber Centre, almost certainly the first DIY store in the district. The business, though now trading under a new name, continues to operate from the same wartime premises.

M.E

Council nurseries in Havant Park, April 1959. Paul Wiseman can be seen on the left, assisting a colleague at the Parks Department nursery.

M.E.

The unforgettable winter of 1963. Happily, it is many years since the snows were as severe as pictured here. Mick Bone, forecourt attendant at Marshall's Havant Garage, has the unenviable task of keeping a clear passage to the pumps! The filling station and garage have since become a major, company-owned, Texaco Service Station. The old Territorial Drill Hall is seen on the left.

November 2001 marked the end of the road for the buildings of Kenwood Employees Social Club in New Lane when the site was cleared for development. The building formerly had been the offices of the Havant Employment Exchange.

D.J.

The Havant Town Mill could claim origins from at least the time of the Conquest. The building pictured dates from the first years of the nineteenth century, however. Milling ceased here in the 1920s and the building was demolished in 1958. The millpond has been almost entirely filled in, and what little is left forms a feature of the grounds of the Dolphin Tavern in Park Road South. A large modern office and car park now occupy the site of the mill.

M.E.

The modern office development, Langstone Gate, was constructed on the site of the old town mill and millpond. The new mill wheel, now captive and, for safety reasons unable to turn, is located just out of view to the right of the building.

D.J.

Prior to clearing the site of the mill itself, the removal of the wheel created a temporary gap in what had long been an important part of local history. The millstream divided here to feed both the wheel and culvert before continuing on its way to provide the power source of the West Mill at Langstone.

M.E.

A new piece of local history was created when, in February 1987, this replica mill wheel was lowered into position in the preserved remains of the mill race alongside the new office development, Langstone Gate. The wheel, four metres in height and weighing 1.5 tonnes, was made by apprentices at The Unicorn Centre in Portsmouth; the cost borne by the Chichester-based Osborne Construction Group.

A sign of the times in which we live and a reminder that production of watercress was once a local industry. The notice is a warning that, whilst watercress can still be found growing wild in several local streams and the remains of the millpond, it would be a grave mistake to consume it or to drink the once pure water – so much for progress!

D.J.

This aerial view includes the cottage homes bearing the unusual title of Potash Terrace, recalling a bygone era. Potash was once an important ingredient in the treatment and curing of hides. Manufactured on an adjacent site, it was an age-old local industry allied to the production of parchment and leather goods.

C.J.B.

Potash Terrace standing derelict awaiting demolition, its last resident having left in the year 2000. Once famously called 'tin-tops' because of their corrugated iron roofs, the cottages were built in 1902 by the owner of the Leigh Park estate, Sir Frederick Fitzwygram, to house estate workers.

J.P.

Havant Garden and Allotment Society's Flower and Vegetable Show, staged annually in Havant Park, included for the first time exhibits from the Poultry Society. Among those in the front row are: C.W. Brian, Councillor Wilson and Mrs Wilson, Mr Dowse and Roy Saunders, Secretary of the Poultry Society.

Members of the Territorial Army Unit of the Royal Artillery perform their drill with what appears to be a three-inch mortar, in February 1958. The location is the old Drill Hall which once occupied a site close to the present Tourist Information Office in Park Road South.

M.E.

On Commonwealth Youth Sunday, the band of the Portsmouth Unit of the Army Cadet Force heads a column of cadets representing Hilsea, Havant, Leigh Park, Horndean and Clanfield, following an inspection in Havant Park. After the inspection and march through the town, a service was held in St Faith's Church.

S.B.

Commonwealth Youth Sunday (second picture).

S.B.

Sharing the scene with members of the Territorial Army are members of the Army Cadet Force undergoing weapons training in the Havant Drill Hall.

S.B.

With building work almost complete, the new Methodist church in Petersfield Road was soon to open its doors to a growing Havant population in 1958.

M.E.

Having achieved borough status in 1974, the need for a new Civic Centre soon became apparent. Commenced in 1976 and completed the following year at a cost of £2,500,000, the new building is seen during construction. To the east of the site are the Police Headquarters and Magistrates Court.

H.B.C.

The impressive building of the Borough Council Offices dominates this view of the administrative centre of the town in 1999. Just in the picture is Havant College, the home of Havant Hockey Club who, in the 1990s, won the National Hockey League title three times.

C.J.B.

The Havant Arms, granted in 1975, are borne by Havant Borough Council under lawful authority by the Earl Marshal delegated to the College of Arms. The extract from the Letters Patent which bears witness to this is worded as follows:

We the said Garter, Clarenceux and Norrey and Ulster Kings of Arms have to these Presents subscribed Our names and affixed Seals of Our several offices this 25th day of March in the twenty-fourth year of the Reign of Our Sovereign Lady Elizabeth the Second by the Grace of God of the United Kingdom of Great Britain and Northern Ireland and of her other realms and territories Queen, Head of the Commonwealth, Defender of the Faith and in the year of our Lord one thousand nine hundred and seventy-five.

H.B.C.

There is no doubt that with the building of the vast Leigh Park estate and other local projects since the war years, Havant was at one time the fastest growing town in England. Now perhaps overtaken by other towns, the population explosion of the Borough of Havant was nonetheless impressive; rising from below 35,000 in 1950 to 110,000 in 1974.

H.B.C.

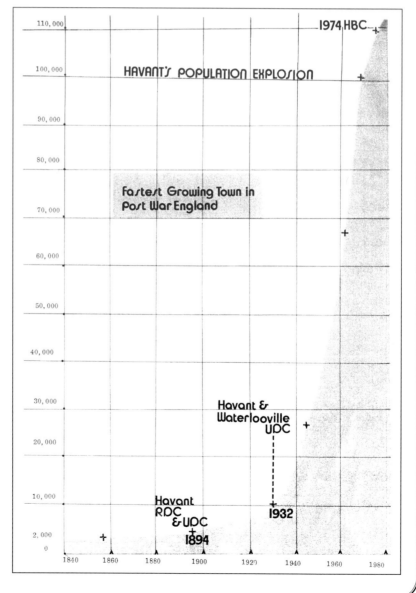

Tessa June Daines was appointed Mayor of the borough in 1985. First elected to serve as member for the Emsworth Ward in 1978, she retired from council service in 1994. During her mayoral year, Mrs Daines emphasised the role of children, which coincided with the International Year of Youth. During sixteen years service as a borough councillor, Mrs Daines was highly regarded by her contemporaries as possessing great ability to solve problems for her constituents and for her good-humoured and kindly approach.

T.D.

Members of Havant Light Opera Company performed in the Council Chambers on several occasions. They are pictured here in 1985, when the programme included their concert version of Gilbert and Sullivan's shortest operetta, 'Trial By Jury'.

S.H.

An important day in the lives of five-year-old Abigail Priestland and Olivia Jordan as they attend school for the first time, in April 1992. In a reorganisation in September 1994, Fairfield First School adopted the title of Fairfield Infants' School.

J.D.

Now tastefully restored by electronics company Snell & Wilcox, Southleigh House is one of the few 'grand' houses to have been spared the attention of the developer. Originally called Woodlands and built in 1820, the house was, for more than sixty years, the home of the White family. Bought in 1903 by Sir Woolmer White, the son of Major Timothy White of multiple chemist fame, the property remained in the family until it was purchased by the Plessey Electronics Company in 1969. When the Plessey Siemens Group vacated the site in the 1990s the property was then acquired by Snell & Wilcox as their headquarters.

This view of Havant, dated 1999, reveals that the new A27 bypass conveniently divides the industrial heart of Broadmarsh and Brockhampton from the rest of the town. The Hermitage stream is seen flowing into Langstone Harbour close to the sewage works at Budd's Farm. The works, covering a larger acreage than originally intended, now also serves the City of Portsmouth.

C.J.B.

CHAPTER TWO

❧ LANGSTONE ❧ AND HAYLING ISLAND

High tides coupled with gale-force onshore winds create problems for residents, motorists and pedestrians alike. The scene was recorded at the junction of Langstone High Street and the Havant Road in October 1961. The shoreline is 100 yards distant at the end of the High Street.

M.E.

Sharing the photograph with the Royal Oak and neighbouring shore-line cottages in 1958, the Old Mill is seen when the tide is at an average height. Exceptional high tides, however, combined with an onshore wind will sometimes flood these buildings and the neighbouring roads.

M.E.

LANGSTONE QUAY

LANGSTONE WAS AN ACKNOWLEDGED PORT IN FORMER TIMES. UPON OCCASIONS OF GENERAL LEVY AND THE ISSUE OF 'SHIPS ORDERS', THE TOWN OF HAVANT FURNISHED FROM ITS PORT OF LANGSTONE – "ONE SHIPPE OF WAR PROPERLY EQUIPPED FOR THE DEFENCE OF THE REALM". LATTERLY, THE PORT WAS MUCH USED IN THE TRADE OF GRAIN, COAL SHINGLE & FERTILIZER BY THE VARIOUS SAILING BARGES WIHCH BECAME KNOWN AS 'LANGSTONE BARGES'.

RESTORATION OF THE QUAY AND ITS SURROUNDS WAS MADE POSSIBLE IN 1980 WITH FUNDS PROVIDED BY:

HAVANT BOROUGH COUNCIL	SAINSBURY CHARITABLE FUND
HAMPSHIRE COUNTY COUNCIL	WHITBREAD WESSEX LTD.
CIVIC TRUST	G. GALE & CO. LTD.
CHICHESTER HARBOUR CONSERVANCY	SOUTHERN TOURIST BOARD

The ancient quay at Langstone which had been unrecognisable as such for a century or more, was, as the illustration suggests, restored in 1980. Set in the paving adjacent to the car park of the Ship Inn is this dedicated stone slab which although not yet of any great age, is rapidly becoming defaced by the weather and constant traffic movements. Reduced in size, the illustration, is of a 'rubbing' made in 1990.

A.R.

This 1999 photograph shows the present road bridge and remains of the rail link to and from Hayling Island. Following the 1963 closure of the railway and subsequent removal of the track, decay which had already set in, together with the now total lack of maintenance, accelerated rotting of the timber construction leaving only the concrete supporting blocks visible at low water.

C.J.B.

Approaching the new Hayling Bridge at its official opening on 10 September 1956 is Sir Dymoke White of Southleigh Park's coach-and-four. Replacing the old wooden structure first built in 1823 and opened by the Duke of Norfolk in his coach-and-four, this new concrete bridge was given the go-ahead in 1953. It was formally opened by the Minister of Transport's Parliamentary Secretary in the presence of dignitaries from Havant & Waterloo Urban District Council, Hampshire County Council and Portsmouth City Council. Built at a cost of £311,000, the bridge continued with the tradition of collecting tolls.

A.B.

Always a bone of contention, the collection of tolls was finally abolished on 11 April 1960 when the Chairman of Hampshire County Council, Mr Alan Lubbock handed over George IV two-shilling pieces to toll collectors, Messrs Bastin and Scutt. The procession includes a penny-farthing bicycle and other vintage vehicles crossing to celebrate a 'free passage' for the first time since 1823!

This scene was recorded in February 1963 during the most severe winter in the south of England since 1947. The Havant to Hayling train makes its way across an icebound Langstone Harbour in this, its final winter; the rail service to the island was axed in November 1963. At low tide the ice lies on the sea bed and at high water sheet ice floats upon the surface.

The big freeze lasted for two weeks and during this time, in the lower reaches of Langstone Harbour, it was possible to walk on the ice across the sea lake between Milton and the Eastney shore.

High tides, again in October 1961, flood Northney Lane and surrounding fields. The creek separating Hayling Island from the mainland is on the left of the scene, with Chichester Harbour in the distance.

M.E.

Dividing the photograph, is the road from Langstone Bridge where it joins Hayling Island at its junction with the minor road to Northney village. The derelict petrol filling station is awaiting the redevelopment which will convert it into the major Texaco Service Station which now dominates the main route into Hayling. In the years prior to the Second World War (1929 until 1938) the fields behind the service station were home to Air Transport and Sales Ltd, a commercial enterprise which operated pleasure flights to and from other local airfields. The Hayling Island Flying Club was established for a few short years here, ceasing operations at the outbreak of war.

P.W.

When Noel Pycroft retired in 1989 a family tradition of brick making came to an end on Hayling Island. Established here as early as 1901 following a move from Portsmouth, the manufacturing methods remained essentially the same as in those early years. In the photograph, Noel is pictured loading upwards of 70,000 bricks into the drying hacks, one of the final processes in the manufacture.

N.P.

Cleeves Garage in Havant Road, North Hayling. Older motorists will probably remember when the garage had the appearance typical of rural filling
stations everywhere, prior to buyout or takeover by the major oil companies.
At the time of the photograph, 1958, there were virtually no 'oil company
owned' garages or service stations in Britain.

M.E.

A series of aerial photographs taken during the severe drought of 1976 revealed stunning crop marks in the Touncil Field, Hayling Island; marks which closely resembled those sketched and recorded by Telfourd Ely c.1900. A programme of excavations covering the years 1976 to 1978 confirmed that here were the remains of a Romano-British Temple.

Of the few resident personalities who have enriched the history of Hayling Island, none figures more prominently than the late Alexander McKee OBE whose legendary exploits were legion. Perhaps best known for his discovery of Henry VIII's sunken ship *Mary Rose,* he was active in many roles besides. Soldier, adventurer, playwright, broadcaster and author, he is remembered with affection by all who knew him. On 19 July 1996, four years after his death and four-hundred-and-fifty-one years to the day since the sinking of the *Mary Rose,* a last tribute was made by family and friends with the dedication of this remarkable epitaph to his memory. The stone had been recovered from the depths of Hayling Bay by members of the *Mary Rose* Special Branch No. 551 British Sub-Aqua Club.

A further tribute to Alexander McKee was unveiled at the *Mary Rose* Museum in Portsmouth Naval Base in March 1998, attended by family, friends, officials and dedicated members of his diving team. The portrait was, fittingly, executed by his daughter-in-law, Alice McKee, who used old snapshots and a tiny passport photograph to develop this remarkable and enduring likeness. The background includes several McKee book titles and a framed picture of his diving team who, with Alex, made possible the discovery and raising of the *Mary Rose*; surely one of the most important British archaeological events of the twentieth century.

I.M.

75

The Regal (1938 to 1968) was the last of three cinemas to cater for the island's film fans; earlier there had been the Victoria Hall in Beach Road and the Savoy in St Mary's Road. (The Savoy building is now the postal sorting office for Hayling.) Television rang the death knell for many small regional cinemas and many took on another guise as bingo halls in the 1960s. The site of the Regal is now that of the car park at Mengeham.

Their famous dad is out of the picture for once but it is not hard to spot the likeness in this shot from July 1961 when Charlie Chaplin's family spent a holiday at Hayling Island. It is not known if 'Charlie' spent time with them during their stay. To complete the tale and keep the record straight, perhaps a local resident of the time can recall the visit?

M.E.

Pictured in 1964, derelict and deserted, the Hayling railway terminus at South Hayling closed to all rail traffic in November 1963. It soon became a magnet for enthusiasts who systematically stripped the site of 'collectable' railway artefacts. Sadly the once proud station also became a target for vandals who delighted in wrecking the buildings.

Pictured from the air in 1967, the derelict railway goods shed was destined to enjoy a totally new existence. After massive fund-raising and much enthusiastic help from local people, the old building has been successfully converted into a small community theatre, home to the Hayling Island Amateur Dramatic Society.

P.W.

The old goods shed after conversion.

The southern shore of Hayling Island, almost always subjected to onshore winds, bears the brunt (and the scars) of Channel storms. Each winter thousands of tons of sand and shingle are displaced by the ravages of the sea and, whilst the beach defences are continually repaired and replaced, nature returns to win yet again. Pictured is Beach Cottage in 1960.

M.E.

THE EMSWORTH GARAGE

34 HIGH STREET,
EMSWORTH, HANTS

PROPRIETOR: P. S. JOPLING
TELEPHONE: EMSWORTH 2326

APPOINTED
GARAGE

Preston Watson & Co. Ltd.

Wine and Spirit Merchants
Ale, Stout & Cyder Bottlers
Mineral Water Manufacturers

Messes, Canteens, and Clubs supplied

HEAD OFFICE: 12 North Street, HAVANT

TELEPHONE 1180/1

ESTABLISHED 1874

J. G. PARHAM & SONS
Queen Street — EMSWORTH — Hants

High-class
Boat
Builders

Repairs and
Conversions a
speciality—
40 years
experience

CHAPTER THREE
❧ INDUSTRY ❧

For possibly a thousand or more years, the processing of animal skins, or fell-mongering, was important to the prosperity of Havant. Closely associated with the art of parchment making, for which the town is famous, the firm of Alfred Stent & Sons of West Street started manufacturing gloves in 1916. The same site had been used previously in the production of parchment and chamois leather. During the Second World War the company began manufacturing gloves, mittens, flying suits and other leather equipment for the war effort, and Stents employees were considered to be in a 'reserved occupation'. After the war the firm produced a variety of products including such mundane items as paint rollers, these having a sheepskin covering! The company ceased trading in 1960. One of the first stages in production of leather goods is cleaning the skins. They are placed on racks before being dipped into a large vat of acid in a de-greasing process. Frank Rist is seen carrying out this task.

M.E.

The drum shop, where skins – known as pelts – are converted into leather by way of 'tanning' in large revolving drums where they are pummelled in a chrome tanning solution. At the tub, left, is Ernest King, foreman of the department.

M.E.

Colouring leather by spraying are Tom Keens and Mrs Ward. These skins were probably used in the manufacture of lambswool slippers and bootees.

M.E.

Glove production took place in one very large room. Here can be seen the processes from the original stretching and cutting of the skins to the finished glove.

M.E.

In a corner of the factory machinists Mrs Owen and Miss Terry are busy sewing gloves.

M.E.

Founded in Bermondsey in 1861, Tebbit Brothers, chrome tanners, took over the factory buildings in Brockhampton Lane and West Street from Alfred Stent in 1960. Suppliers of leather for the shoe industry, Tebbit Brothers continued with the long tradition of fell-mongering in Havant. The supply of hides arrived each week from East Africa and were 'tanned', treated with chemicals, in huge wooden drums and converted into leather.

M.E.

Mr Douglas West is pictured here testing the thickness of a hide after it has passed through a shaving machine.

M.E.

The leather is dyed black and pasted onto glass panels before being passed through drying machines for six hours. Ted Smith, seen in the foreground, and Robert McConnell are the operatives.

M.E.

Seen working at one of the hydraulic presses is Bill Stemp who had started work in 1928 as an apprentice glove cutter for Stent & Sons at the age of fourteen. Along with other employees of Stents, he was re-employed when Tebbit Brothers took the business over.

M.E.

Mrs G. Whitehouse at work on a hydraulic press.

M.E.

The Minimodels factory in New Lane opened in 1954 and initially produced toys such as Startex and Scalex, these being tin-plate, clockwork models accurately based on cars of the period. Fred Francis, the owner of Minimodels, suggested the idea of Scalextric in 1956 and by Christmas the following year it had become the fastest growing, best-selling toy of the day. In 1958 the company was taken over by Lines Brothers (Triang). Changes included the introduction of the plastic range of cars in 1960 and a move to new premises in Fulflood Road, Leigh Park, in 1961 where the picture records the 'test-bed' layout of cars and track. There followed a gradual running down of the factory until 1970 when Scalextric production was moved to Kent.

In what is probably a promotional photograph, former racing driver, Stirling Moss, employs his expertise on the miniature racing circuit.

I'm Backing Britain

Colt International, Havant 1968. The Colt-inspired 'I'm Backing Britain' campaign was front-page news for several weeks throughout the country. Employers and employees together created a spirit of patriotism not seen since the war years. Lapel badges carrying the slogan and the Union Flag were worn everywhere and, in the Colt factories, employees willingly agreed to work an hour a day without pay. By the end of the year, other news had pushed the campaign to the back pages, although it was still operating under the aegis of the Industrial Society at the end of the year.

J.S.

On 5 May 1977 His Royal Highness Prince Philip, Duke of Edinburgh, made a flying visit to the Colt factory at Havant. His helicopter landed in the grounds of Oak Park School where the Duke was welcomed by headmaster Mr R. Lane before being driven the short distance to the Colt Works.

J.S.

Arriving at Colt, Prince Philip was met by managing director Mr I.J. O'Hea before touring the works and meeting staff and executives. It was a case of many happy returns, as this was the third time that Prince Philip and Mr O'Hea had met.

J.S.

Internationally famous for the manufacture of innovative quality yacht fittings, the Lewmar Marine Company is a world leader in a highly competitive market. In recognition of such achievement, this Havant-based company was, in 1985, presented with The Queen's Award For Industry. The presentation, made by the Lord Lieutenant of Hampshire, was an occasion that demanded the presence of the entire workforce to share the honour with Mr John Burton, company director.

Dominating the skyline for twenty-three years, the much maligned incinerator was finally demolished in September 1997 after failing to meet European guidelines. The Havant burner was opened in 1974 and, on average, burned 60,000 tonnes of waste from Portsmouth, Havant and East Hampshire each year. Prior to its closure, an environmental group, 'Residents Against the Burner', had campaigned vigorously against its further use.

D.J.

CHAPTER FOUR
❧ THE RAILWAY SCENE ❧

Circus Special.   In December 1957 the Trosnant School Parent-Teacher
Association, always forward thinking and innovative, organised an extra-
special Christmas trip with a visit to Bertram Mills Circus at Earls Court,
London.   The day was made all the more memorable with the provision of
a seasonably decorated excursion train.   The excited children are seen
waiting to board at Havant Railway Station.

M.E.

Another railway occasion recorded at Havant was the January 1959 excursion to celebrate the centenary of the Direct Line London to Portsmouth. It was certainly a day to remember for railway enthusiasts who eagerly await the arrival of this vintage locomotive.

M.E.

The Havant to Hayling Line. Having left Havant Station, passing under the East Street bridge (which still carries road transport), the train is seen on a section of track which, with railside banks removed, is now the car park of Town End House, Havant Museum and Arts Centre.

M.E.

At Havant Road Crossing and approaching Langstone Halt, manually operated gates restricted road traffic from each direction. With the ever increasing volume of traffic and queues, often stretching for hundreds of yards, the problem became a deciding factor in the decision to close the line.

M.E.

Hayling Railway Bridge. Of particular interest from an engineering and railway enthusiast point of view, the following photographs illustrate the largely Victorian construction. The bridge was required to allow access for shipping between the two harbours of Langstone and Chichester. A 30ft-gap could be created, as in this instance, the through passage of a sailing barge.

The mechanism to operate the swing section needed a team of three people to work the capstan-like device and seen in action here are Charlie Semple, Ron Stilwell and Fred Church. After disconnecting the signal wires and removing the 32 bolts holding the fish plates on the running rails, the lines-men together with the Langstone Bridge signalman, open the bridge by means of the capstan bar, turning the swing span through 90 degrees in a clockwise direction. A flag or lamp on the adjacent shipping mast indicated when a vessel could pass through the channel.

A.B

In a photograph taken from sea-level, it is possible to see the maintenance gallery and principal driving gear of the mechanism.

A.B.

This picture from immediately below shows the rack and pinion gearing and roller race.

A.B.

Finally, with the bridge dismantled and rails and decking removed, it is possible to see the immense turntable which propelled the swing section.

H.B.C.

West side looking north and photographed from the Hayling shore, the 1000ft-long structure is seen to have its timbers supported upon massive concrete blocks. In the year 2002 these blocks are the only visible evidence left to show that the Hayling Railway ever crossed the harbour.

A.B.

In May 1966 Portsmouth-based brewers Brickwoods opened the uniquely named Hayling Billy public house on Hayling Island. The interior was designed like carriage furnishings and Brickwoods carried on the theme by purchasing a redundant Terrier steam locomotive from its last active location on the Meon Valley Line to be installed in the car park. Repainted in its original livery of 'Stroudley's improved Terrier green' it was given its original name of 'Newington'. Several years later, with the sellout of Brickwoods to brewing giants Whitbread, the 'Newington' was given to the Haven Street Railway on the Isle of Wight where, in a livery of Southern Railway green, it continues to run regularly under its new name, 'Freshwater'.

A.B.

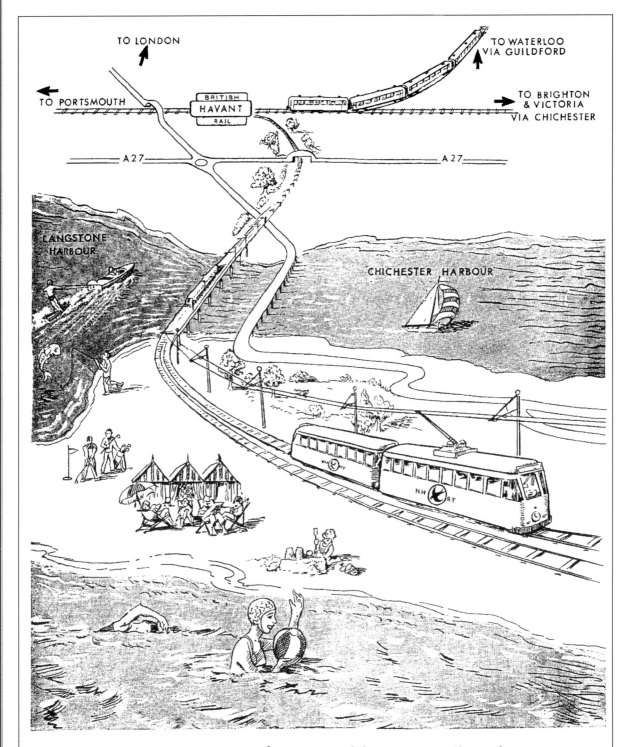

Hayling Light Railway Society

Plans were already in hand prior to closure, to revive the Havant to Hayling line with an electric-powered system employing a redundant/surplus tram from the Blackpool Corporation Tramway. A new company, The Hayling Light Railway Company, was formed with the intention of providing a service powered by overhead lines throughout the route.

The Blackpool tram was successfully transported to Havant where it negotiated a difficult route through West Street.

A.B.

The low-load articulated transporter is seen here turning into Park Road North, with perhaps the most arduous section of its journey yet to come.

A.B.

Arriving at the goods yard, the tram was manhandled to a safe position from where it could be placed in a vacant siding to await what proved to be an uncertain future. In the event, the dream of a revived Havant to Hayling Railway failed, probably because plans to create a major Havant bypass would have presented insurmountable civil engineering problems on the proposed route.

A.B.

CHAPTER FIVE

↜ BEDHAMPTON ↝
AND PORTSDOWN

In 1921, pioneering archaeologist O.G.S. Crawford examined and recorded the remains of a Roman Road in Bedhampton. Reckoned to be part of the route from Chichester to Bitterne, the road then crossed Purbrook Heath and could be traced in a straight line to Wickham. But it was not until October 1953 that a section was again investigated at Bedhampton. Arthur (Bill) Corney of Portsmouth City Museums is pictured when the surface was again revealed, assessed and measured. Further information relating to the subject may be found in the Resources and Local Studies Room at Havant Museum.

R.F.

The central timber-framed portion of Bedhampton Manor House probably dates to the early seventeenth century, but the brick-built wings are 'Victorian Tudor'. The manor house, now a retirement home, may well stand on the site of the 'hall' referred to in the Domesday Book.

J.P.

Originally built as a granary and store, the building has recently been converted into living accommodation. Rumoured to have been owned by a nearby mill that produced biscuits for the Navy, it has also seen use as a squash court until its conversion to a family home.

R.C.

Yet one more landmark disappeared from the local horizon in March 1962, when Portsmouth Water Company decided to topple the Brockhampton Works chimney. Opened in 1889, it became a standby station in 1927. This and the major chimney at the Havant Works became redundant when coal was discontinued as the principal source of power.

M.E.

North Street, Bedhampton, photographed in 1957. The street, then little more than a lane leading from Bedhampton Road to Hooks Lane, has since changed beyond recognition; each of the properties pictured has since been replaced with modern housing.

A.B.

A scene that has changed dramatically over the years is captured on a busy day in September 1959. For more than eighty years Coldman's General Stores served the inhabitants of Bedhampton until its closure in October 1971. Seen on the left of the photograph, the family-run store stood at the corner of Bedhampton Hill Road and Brookside Road. To the right was the old Belmont Tavern on the junction of the road leading to Portsdown Hill. Demolished in the 1960s, another public house bearing the same name was later built a little further to the east.

M.E.

When West End Post Office closed in July 1963, it brought to an end a family tradition of service which the public had enjoyed for eighty-three years. The last postmistress, Miss Dorothy Shepperd, bowed out after forty years, a record only surpassed by her father who had held the position for forty-three years. The town also suffered the loss of its Victorian post box which was one of only two surviving examples in the area.

M.E.

Bedhampton 1957. Photographed from the 'Goatfield' bridge opposite Cromwell Terrace, the view includes the premises of Brown's the Butcher who ceased trading many years ago. The Primitive Methodist chapel, built in 1878 and sited close to the railway line, has since been demolished after spending its last years as a wholesale warehouse.

A.B.

The volume of traffic has changed little as vehicles await the passing of a train at the Bedhampton crossing gates in the late 1950s. Later road widening of West Street into New Road involved the destruction of properties on the left of the picture.

R.C.

September 1974 saw the removal of the old crossing gates and the installation of Continental-style, automatic barriers; this section of West Street was closed to all traffic during this period. Five years later, in May 1979, the crossing keeper's box, seen top left, was removed.

M.E.

The lone fir tree survived several road improvements to provide a landmark and local 'signpost' at the junction of roads leading to both upper and lower Bedhampton. Located at the eastern end of the 40-acre field, it proved an invaluable navigational aid to locals and strangers alike until it was felled to allow the construction of approach roads to and from the A3M motorway. An untidy specimen, perhaps, the loss was lamented as that of an old friend. The photograph is dated 1958.

M.E.

Bedhampton Church Hall was built upon the site of the former sickbay of the Bedhampton Royal Naval Camp. The foundation stone ceremony was performed in June 1958, the main hall and the St Nicholas Sanctuary opening in 1959 at a total cost of £14,000. The new hall was built nearer to the centre of the parish, providing a venue for parish activities and serving the community in general.

M.E.

Bedhampton Road photographed on a quiet day in 1957. The Home Stores grocers, (formerly the Wheelwrights public house) and Newell's Garage share the terrace with the Gospel Hall and the Golden Lion public house. The Home Stores were later converted into a Tyre Sales and Motor Repair Centre.

A.B.

Brockhampton Stream, in the foreground, has its source in springs in the grounds of Portsmouth Water plc, south of West Street, Havant. This may have been the Saxon Ocerburna which once formed the boundary between Havant and Bedhampton. The scene is dominated by the towering installations of the gravel quay on Storehouse Lake.

J.P.

The Bedhampton and District Poultry Society stage a special event at the newly opened Warblington School in 1955. Among those pictured are Councillor Powell, Chairman of Havant and Waterloo UDC, Councillor Olding and, seated centre, Ralph Wightman BBC broadcaster and farming expert.

M.E.

Recorded in May 1963, the scene is of the western edge of Bedhampton, taken at an altitude of 10,000 feet. Though the landscape appears perfectly flat, in reality, you are looking at the eastern end of the Portsdown with the hill slopes running away in each direction. The white scar in the chalk is all that remains of the Farlington Redoubt, while, to its left, is the unique shield-shape of the copse known locally as 'dead man's wood', alongside the once tortuous route of the original Crookhorn Lane. Top left of the picture is Morelands anti-aircraft site, with huts and gun pits still in evidence.

This superb 1977 aerial photograph of the Crookhorn development encompasses the housing estate, golf course, Southdowns College, the fringes of both Widley and Purbrook (all on the northern slopes of Portsdown Hill), as well as, at the top of the picture, Leigh Park and parts of Bedhampton.

To alleviate the traffic problems caused by the tortuous, winding ascent of Crookhorn Lane, the decision was made in 1971, to cut through the Portsdown, abandon the old lane, and so provide a more direct route from the Portsdown Hill Road to Crookhorn, Purbrook and beyond.

H.B.C.

This second photograph was taken shortly after its official opening and before the exposed chalk slowly became hidden beneath a verdant covering, a process which is still ongoing after thirty years.

H.B.C.

The Bevis Grave, Portsdown. Originally the location of a ploughed-out Neolithic long barrow, the site was investigated and excavated between 1974 and 1976. The team of professional archaeologists were assisted by students from Havant College, pictured surface-digging and passing the soil through fine sieves before consigning it to the spoil heap.

R.F.

Work carried out in the first season revealed traces of an extensive Anglo-Saxon Christian cemetery containing a total of 88 skeletons, each burial aligned east/west. Two burials discovered at the west end of a Neolithic ditch and buried north/south were attributed to the pagan period.

R.F.

Perhaps your ancestor or mine? The date of these Saxon burials has been placed between the seventh and early ninth centuries AD. At a date some time before 1817, another three inhumations, accompanied by a broken spear, were found in the course of chalk digging (Butler, 1817). The figure 225 displayed by the grave refers only to the site reference and not to how many skeletons had been uncovered. Contemporary archaeologists assume the majority of the burials to have been associated with the neighbouring settlement of Bedhampton.

R.F.

CHAPTER SIX
❧ LEIGH PARK ❧
OLD AND NEW

Leigh Park Farmhouse 1998. Now the tea-room of Staunton Country Park, the farmhouse and outbuildings had originally been part of the settlement which had grown around the first Leigh Park House. Incorporated into the estate by William Garrett when he acquired the site in 1800, the farmhouse probably dates from the middle of the eighteenth century. Though recognised as an ornamental farm it was, nevertheless, a working farm with a dairy, cheese-room and buttery attached. Renovation work carried out at the country park has transformed the building back to its original design and it is now a popular stopping-off point for visitors to the farm trail.

The Gothic Library was originally built as an extension to the first Leigh Park House by Sir George Staunton in 1832 in the style of a Gothic chapter house, to accommodate his collection of more than 300 Chinese books. When Staunton's mansion was demolished in the mid-1860s after William Stone built the second Leigh Park House, the library remained as a reminder of bygone days. The stained glass windows above the bookcases, depicting Staunton family members, were removed for safe keeping during the war and, curiously, lost. The library now forms part of the Staunton Country Park and is used as an interpretation centre devoted to the history of the estate.

Above and below: Staunton Country Park 1994. Declared open by the Duke of Gloucester, the large glasshouse within the walled garden of the country park had been built to the original design of Sir George. It now houses a fine collection of exotic plants including palms, bananas and the giant Amazon waterlily.

A winter's day is captured in these two fine 1980s photographs of the Chinese Bridge and the lake in Leigh Park Gardens.

Winter in Leigh Park Gardens.

Leigh Park House, pictured shortly before demolition in June 1958, was built in the early 1860s by William Henry Stone soon after he acquired the Leigh Park estate from the family of Sir George Thomas Staunton. The house, designed in the Gothic style, was built from bricks made on the estate.

The house and grounds were requisitioned in 1940 – and occupied until 1956 – by the Admiralty Mine Design Department. The house and park land were then handed over to Portsmouth City Council which had earlier purchased the house and grounds in 1944. By 1956, 150 acres of parkland and gardens around the house were in use as public open space. But Portsmouth City Council's attempts to find an organisation to take over and use the house were to no avail. In the face of prohibitive maintenance expenses after years of neglect, the decision was taken to demolish the house and this was completed in June 1959.

M.E.

The Terrace, with its fine views overlooking the lake, is now the only reminder of days when the second Leigh Park House dominated the landscape. When the house was demolished in June 1959 the Terrace remained as a feature of the gardens.

Always a target for vandals, as the photograph of 1997 shows, the Terrace is earmarked to be rebuilt under a current restoration programme.

Once part of an estate that comprised 16 farms until they were all sold off in 1936, Middle Park Farmhouse stood on Park Lane, once the road from Bedhampton to Cowplain. One of the largest of the former farms, the land comprised 196 acres, some of which is still farmed today. The farmhouse was eventually demolished in the early 1960s to make way for the development of the Warren housing estate.

Dunsbury Hill Farm, the largest of the estate farms, comprised 237 acres of which a surprising area of land remains undeveloped. The farmhouse was once advertised as a 'Gentleman's Residence' in the sale of 1936, and stood close to what is now the A3M motorway until its removal in 1996. Together with nearby Middle Park Farm, the Whitbread family were the owners for many years.

Soon after work had started on the construction of Wakefords School (now Staunton Park) in West Leigh, Havant, in 1967, important evidence of Roman occupation was discovered. During the excavation of a small Roman building by Portsmouth City Museums, a cameo was found just below the surface and can now be seen in their collection.

The Leigh Park housing estate with Bramdean Drive under construction in 1948. The wartime bombing of Portsmouth caused massive destruction of properties and left many people homeless; coupled with a serious pre-war housing problem, swift action was needed to overcome the problem. In February 1943, thanks mainly to Councillor F.G.H. Storey, recommendations were made for the purchase by Portsmouth City Council of the former Leigh Park estate. Work commenced on building the new council estate in 1947, with Bramdean Drive being the first to be completed.

Building work on the estate was carried on throughout the 1950s, with families moving in as soon as each property was completed. In the very early days of the estate there were few roads, shops or other amenities – nothing but a gigantic building site surrounded by countryside. The photograph shows Corhampton Crescent shortly after completion, with Purbrook Way forming the background.

Park Parade. A rapidly expanding housing estate soon demanded more facilities, and shops were quickly built to serve the needs of an increasing population. Begun in 1955, with the Co-operative Department Store the first to open its doors in November of that year, by 1958 Park Parade boasted more than 40 shops. On the left of the picture can be seen the News Agency, Gas Company Showroom and Pinks the grocer.

Park Parade, the main shopping centre of the Leigh Park estate was begun in 1955. The photograph, dated 1958, shows the Post Office, which still survives, and other early shops such as Maynards (confectioners), the London Central Meat Company and Monty Gaiman (grocers). By 1966 the opening of the Greywell Precinct to the north of Park Parade added further shops and facilities.

Map showing the ten-year plan for the development of the housing estate.

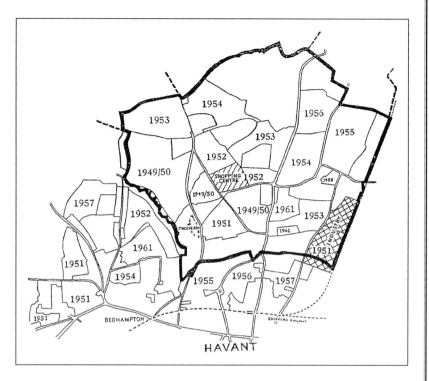

St Francis was the first purpose-built church on Leigh Park estate. Before this, services were held in a prefabricated hall at the rear of the new church. As can be seen, the then Archdeacon of Portsmouth, the Venerable Michael Peck, laid the foundation stone of the church on 25 November 1962. The new church was consecrated by the Bishop of Portsmouth, Dr John Phillips, on 30 November 1963.

M.E.

Riders Lane, an ancient droveway linking the woodland pastures of Havant Thicket and the Forest of Bere with the hamlet of Bedhampton, survives miraculously amidst the bricks and mortar of Leigh Park housing estate. The great width of the grassy track is still measured by the line of oaks which flank it. The trees to the left of the photograph once defined the boundary of Bedhampton's medieval deer park.

J.P.

By 1952 the growth of Leigh Park had made the Havant Parish of St Joseph's too large for one priest, and a curate was sent to work with the growing numbers of Roman Catholics in the area. The first church was an ex-Royal Navy Nissen hut on Middle Park Way between Swanmore Road and Winterslow Drive. In 1954 the site of the new church was purchased on the corner of Dunsbury Way and Bramdean Drive. The first Mass was performed on Christmas Eve 1954 in a new building, named after the Blessed Margaret Pole, which would eventually become the church hall. In 1966 Leigh Park became a parish in its own right and it was agreed that a new church should be built on the site. A legacy of £21,000 was donated by an unknown lady for the construction of the new church, on condition that it should be named St Michael and All Angels. On 15 May 1970 the Bishop of Portsmouth, the Rt Revd Mgr. Derek Worlock, officially blessed and opened the new building. After serving the Catholic community for more than thirty years, the church was sadly destroyed by fire and eventually demolished. Services were subsequently carried out in the Church of St Francis in Riders Lane.

P.H.

This view of Dunsbury Way shows the ill-fated St Michael and All Angels Catholic Church situated on the corner of Bramdean Drive. On 5 July 2001 a bolt of lightning blasted through the roof, turning the building into a blazing inferno. Seventy fire-fighters tackled the blaze but, unfortunately, the church could not be saved and was later demolished.

C.J.B.

The busy shopping centres of Park Parade and the Greywell Precinct dominate this 1999 view of the centre of Leigh Park. Close at hand, the library, community centre and bingo hall all combine to make this a focal point of the sprawling estate.

C.J.B.

The green belt between Leigh Park and Waterlooville has been steadily eroded by the increased development that has taken place since this scene was recorded in the 1980s. The A3M motorway is seen cutting a swathe through the picture to the north of the former Havant Hypermarket.

C.J.B.

CHAPTER SEVEN
❧ SPORT ❧

Founded in 1951, Havant Rugby Club has gone from strength to strength during its fifty-year history. The club came to its present home at Hooks Lane in 1953, with the clubhouse, built by members, opening two years later. Since the early 1970s, Havant has been a regular winner of the Hampshire Cup and became the first junior club to go into the National John Player Cup. Entering the National League in 1987, it reached the top of National League Division Three in 1992/3, just missing promotion to Division Two on points difference. The photograph shows the first club team in the season 1951/52.

Invited guests at the Trosnant School swimming gala 1962 included Portsmouth Football Club celebrities (from left) Tony Barton, Harry Harris, David Dodson and Alex Wilson. The pool was the result of fund-raising and hard physical work by the Parent-Teacher Association, headmaster John Hunt (himself a former Football League referee) and the staff.

Trosnant School Football Team 1962–63. With its headmaster's sporting pedigree, it was not surprising that the junior school achieved a reputation in the late 1950s and 1960s for producing winning teams in both football and netball. Posing with the camera with Mr Hunt (back row, far right) and the school's sports master, the team displays its trophies won in this season.

Trosnant School Netball Team 1964–65 are all smiles for the camera as they pose proudly with their own shield, having achieved a sporting double for the school. It means another camera call for Mr Hunt, this time with the school's sports mistress.

Efforts to discover more about this young man have failed to reveal anything more than him being Havant Swimming Pool's 100,000th visitor in October 1974, when he was handed his locker key, as shown in this photograph. The pool opened its doors to the public on 23 May 1974.

H.B.C.

Presumably an award of free entry to the pool was presented but borough archives and museum resources have, so far, been unable to determine the identity of the boy or that of his companions; the hope is that someone will be able to offer more information.

H.B.C.

Above and opposite: Most of us associate the sport of sailboarding with the west coast of the USA but it actually began on Hayling Island. During the summer of 1958 Peter Chilvers, then a schoolboy aged twelve, began experimenting with a piece of plywood, a tent fly sheet, some curtain rings and an old wooden pole.

Peter eventually went into full-time production of sailboards and even successfully sued the American Wind Surfing International over patent infringements. The three photographs demonstrate the preparation for and skill involved in the sport.

P.W.

The Tour de France passing through Havant on 7 July 1994 brought out the crowds for a memorable day. In addition to the hundreds of participants, publicity caravans, trade and manufacturers' vehicles carrying reserve bicycles, and both French and British motorcycle police (some performing 'wheelies' and handstands!) added to the colourful spectacle. The day's event commenced and finished at Portsmouth, covering 113 miles in an average time of four hours thirty minutes.

Spectators lining the route congregate on the pavements, eager to get a good view of the cyclists whizzing through. The notice displays the fact that both carriageways of the Rowlands Castle to Havant road are to be closed to traffic until the cavalcade has safely passed.

The decision to amalgamate the two principal football teams in the borough into one new club was taken in 1998. Both Havant Town FC and Waterlooville FC were clubs which, despite having great ambition and reasonable success, were finding it difficult to make it to the elite of non-league football. Income from home games was low, with poor attendances owing to their grounds being just a few miles apart. Waterlooville sold its Jubilee Park Ground to pay off mounting debts while Havant's ground at West Leigh received a facelift, and after the formal merger on 1 June 1998, the new club looked to the future with optimism. Now doing well in the Dr Marten's League the team is pressing for promotion into the Conference League, with the Football League its ultimate goal. Havant Town FC line up for the camera in the season 1985/86 at West Leigh. Back row, from left: S. Pope, K. Rapley, B. Hewett, M. Jacob, M. Spencer, T. Morris, T. Plumbley, S. McIntyre, C. Hancock. Front row, from left: M. Aldworth, S. Smith, A. Plumbley, G. Blaylock, G. Galaway, C. Boyes.

A.G.

Season 2001-2002. With a mixture of home-grown talent and seasoned professionals from Portsmouth and other football league clubs, Havant and Waterlooville FC have become one of the regions top non-league clubs. Lining up for the pre-season team photograph, player-manager Liam Daish and his squad pose in front of the newly refurbished stand at West Leigh Park.

A.G.

Founded in 1902, the Avenue Lawn Tennis and Squash Club of Warblington proudly celebrates its centenary. From its original four, leased, public courts in Havant Recreation Ground, the club progressed to its own present location in 1920. Now boasting ten grass and seven hard courts, additional facilities include three squash courts and a fitness room. There is also a modern clubhouse with a comfortable lounge and fully licensed bar for members and visitors. Pictured on a less busy afternoon, members enjoy watching a singles match. Voted the Lawn Tennis Association Club of 1996, the club looks forward to a successful future.

E.U.

Winner of the Avenue Open Tournament in 1989, Christopher Wilkinson repeated his success in 1999 and is seen being presented with his trophy by the club president Alan Sherwood. Experience at 'club tennis' level, was indeed the spur for Chris to achieve his ambition and compete on the hallowed courts of Wimbledon.

S.S.

The Seacourt Tennis Club in Hayling Island is renowned for being the only club in the world where all of the five recognised racket games are played: Real Tennis, Lawn Tennis, Badminton, Squash and Rackets. On its completion in 1980, the Rackets court was declared open for play on 6 June by world-class cricketer Colin Cowdrey. Sharing the memorable occasion are five World Rackets Champions. From left: William Surtees, John Prenn, Jim Dear, Geoffrey Atkins and Howard Angus.

D.M.

Members and guests crowd the court and viewing gallery, all anxious to be a part of this unforgettable day.

D.M.

Ned Danby (right), founder of the Seacourt Club, shares a moment with Colin Cowdrey on one of several occasions when the scheduled tournament was sponsored by the Unigate Company.

D.M.

CHAPTER EIGHT

WATERLOOVILLE

No longer part of the local scene in Cowplain, Fodens had operated from these London Road premises, following an earlier move from Albert Road, Cosham, until the 1960s when the site became the location of Waitrose. Of undoubted interest to tram and railway enthusiasts, the second photograph (*below*) shows the same building when it was the Cowplain depot and tram shed of the Portsdown and Horndean Light Railway c.1930.

The original church of St George's, Waterlooville, was built in 1831 to serve the small community that had established itself around the crossroads of London, Hambledon and Stakes Hill in Waterlooville.

Built from funds raised by subscription from various local landowners such as Thomas Thistlethwaite and John Hulbert, the church, built in the Gothic style, was consecrated on 26 January 1831 by the Vicar General, the Revd William Dealty D.D. After serving a growing population for more than one-hundred-and-thirty years, it was decided that the small church needed either replacing or enlarging. Several plans were considered before a decision was reached to build a new church, but retaining almost half of the original building including the chancel and altar. The old tower was completely re-faced and a spacious nave added. The new church was greeted with widespread approval and great credit to the architect Mr Ken Makins. The new edifice was re-hallowed by the Bishop of Portsmouth, the Rt Revd John Phillips, in April 1970.

Wadham Brothers, Waterlooville. Established in 1905 by brothers Harold and Wilfred, the business began by selling, hiring and maintaining motor cars. Trade rapidly increased and additional premises were opened in both the London and Hambledon Road. Although the company has now ceased trading, the business went through several periods of expansion, trading as Wadham Stringer and Wadham Kenning before closure of its base in Waterlooville.

An important side of the business since 1910 had been designing cars, vans, buses and ambulance bodies for customers at home and abroad. The two photographs show the Wadham showrooms in Hambledon Road between 1958 and 1968.

Yet another example of the planners' zeal to redevelop existing properties and their land was the demolition of Rockville in 1962. This fine building, once the home of Lord Mayor of Portsmouth Sir Dennis Daley, and Lady Daley, caught fire during its demolition and was burned out on 3 July 1962. The site was eventually used for the construction of modern housing in what is now Gloucester Road.

D.W.

Stakes Hill Lodge, home of the Hulbert family for more than one-hundred-and-fifty years, suffered an ignominious end in a disastrous fire on 18 June 1973. Built originally in 1820 by John Spice Hulbert, the estate was home to the family who gave us the legacy of Hulbert Road, until the estate was sold acrimoniously in February 1973. With the need for additional housing and space for the proposed A3M motorway, Havant and Waterloo District Council and the Greater London Council each had a wish to purchase the estate. In the event the land, less the house, was finally purchased by Havant and Waterloo District Council, with the previous owner's assurance that the property would be retained but, as already mentioned, the house was later destroyed by fire.

H.B.C.

Broadlands Mansion, Waterlooville, is probably best remembered first as catering specialists and then a garden centre. The mansion was built c.1890 by George Hulbert of Stakes Hill Lodge for one of his spinster daughters, and the estate of eleven acres was originally called The Willows. For a period both before and after the Great War, it was the home of Rear-Admiral Sir Reginald Tyrwhitt. During the 1930s it became an hotel and in the 1950s a garden centre. All traces of mansion and garden had been removed by 1982 and the site since redeveloped as the base for a superstore and DIY centre.

Above and opposite: A notice in a local newspaper suggesting the formation of a musical society resulted in Waterlooville Musical Players being formed in September 1969. The level of response and enthusiasm meant it was possible to choose Gilbert and Sullivan's 'The Mikado' as a first production. In May 1970, just eight months after the initial meeting, 'The Mikado' was staged to great acclaim at the Hart Plain School. No one could ever imagine that from such small beginnings, the company was to appear many times in the future on the professional stage of the King's Theatre, Southsea.

CAST

THE MIKADO OF JAPAN	PETER ROGERS
NANKI-POO	JOHN KENT
KO-KO	TED MARSH
POOH-BAH	BILL SNELLING
PISH-TUSH	ALFRED SIMS
YUM-YUM	JEAN NORRIS
PEEP-BO	GWEN PEOPALL
KATISHA	MARION SMITH
PITTI-SING	ROSEMARY MURPHY

THE CHILDREN

AMANDA SMITH, JANE HIGGINBOTTOM, FABIA SMITH,
STEVEN HIGGINBOTTOM, DEBORAH ROUTLEY,
KIM WALSH & KATHRYN ROUTLEY

MENS CHORUS

DAVID SELVIDGE, MAURICE FRANKS, RON NORRIS
DOUGLAS WHITE, IAN WHITE, JOHN JEFFERS
IVOR FEBEN, WILLIAM PRATT, EMLYN PARRY
ALBERT HIDEMAN

LADIES CHORUS:- WINIFRED HICKMAN, VICKIE WEST
MARILYN MAYNARD, NORAH WHAMOND, KATHLEEN HOLE
HELENA HOWES, ROSE BERTRAM, LUCY WARREN, JUNE
FRANKS, EILEEN SCROGGINS, ROSEMARY FALLICK, ANN
PEARSON, JOANNE SOAL, ELEANOR BATCHELOR, MOLLIE
WHITE, ANNETTE ROUTLEY, PATRICIA WHITE.

****

145

Members of the Waterlooville Musical Players visited HMS *Victory* at Portsmouth in September 1976, to pose for this publicity photograph for their forthcoming production of 'HMS Pinafore' at the King's Theatre, Southsea. Cast members pictured are, from left: Suzanne Weston, Carol Viner, Mary Kidd, Sue Watson, John Batten, Bryan Baber and Steve Chivers.

Sir Alec Rose was knighted by Her Majesty Queen Elizabeth II, following his epic solo round-the-world voyage. The Portsmouth grocer later retired to Havant and, among his many charitable interests, became President of the Hampshire Rose Lifeboat Appeal. It is in this role that he is pictured with Paddy Flynn, Chairman of the Waterlooville Lions Club, and Jack Wigg, Chairman of the Waterlooville Musical Players, receiving a cheque on behalf of the Lions Club who in 1974 sponsored the Players' performance of Gilbert and Sullivan's 'Yeoman Of The Guard' at the King's Theatre, Southsea.

Waterlooville shopping in the 1970s. Traffic negotiates the cross-roads before pedestrianisation of the London Road in 1985.

H.B.C.

Traffic-free precincts are now the future for the modern shopper; all is safer, cleaner and far more pleasant, now that this section of the London Road has been updated.

H.B.C.

With a fountain as its centrepiece, this pedestrianised section of the London Road was officially declared open by the Mayor of Havant, Councillor Ken Moss on 4 May 1985.

H.B.C.

The changing face of the town centre is recorded in this aerial view of 1999. Possibly far more than any other part of the borough, Waterlooville has developed beyond recognition (and people's memories) in the past twenty years. A mixture of commerce, industry and the need for more housing has transformed the district from its rural beginnings into the fastest growing area of the borough.

C.J.B.

A one-time location of St Peter's Roman Catholic Primary School, and since used for various social welfare activities, the former site of the convent is still dominated by the Church of the Sacred Heart. The front of the convent, built in 1894, remains unchanged whilst other buildings are now derelict. Downland Housing Association purchased several of the buildings in 1985 to provide sheltered accommodation for the elderly.

C.J.B.

CHAPTER NINE

❧ EMSWORTH ❧

Emsworth oyster fishermen Charles Treagust and Jack Savage display their catch, December 1961.

M.E.

Emsworth staged a Water Carnival for more than fifty years but the 1953 event was celebrated with more than the usual enthusiasm, albeit some two months after the coronation; even royalty have to bow to time and tide tables! The programme lists events, competitions, public service timetables and potted histories of local noteworthy places. Part sponsored by local businessmen, it also included drawings, photographs, illustrations and a number of advertisements which, after a fifty-year gap, leave us to recall, perhaps, the names of companies no longer trading.

The Emsworth British Legion and community lost a valuable facility when the club burned down in April 1962. Mainly constructed of timber, little was left despite the efforts of the fire brigade who had only to come from across North Street. The club possessed a large hall with a stage, dressing rooms, billiard room, bar and the Legion club room.

M.E.

'Dusty' Miller of Emsworth displays the latest in black and white television and Bakelite-clad radio sets on his trade stand at the Chamber Of Commerce Exhibition, Havant 1957.

M.E.

Emsworth Tufty Club. Who among our readers recalls the 1960s nationwide scheme to instruct and educate the under-fives in road safety? Extensive television, magazine and newspaper campaigns and demonstrations made 'Tufty the squirrel' a household name. Tufty indicates, from within his display case, that demonstrations will take place in the Public Hall, North Street.

H.B.C.

With a canvas zebra-crossing to simulate the real thing, Emsworth children, with mums and grannies, receive instruction in how to cross the road safely.

H.B.C.

South Street, Emsworth, and a chance to have all your motoring problems resolved whilst browsing for that desirable antique. The garage later specialised in the restoration of older vehicles and the antiques business reverted to being a house once again.

P.B.

The building to the right of the previous picture survives today in a more elegant guise, that of The Book Shop, catering for all tastes and ages. The building being gable-end onto the road may show that the site, if not the building itself, is of greater age than the adjacent properties.

P.B.

Emsworth High Street. The style of the modern buildings blends well with the older architecture, allowing the Crown Hotel to project onto the pavement. The previous shops on this site were demolished following a fire on 30 September 1960 which, fuelled by the flammable stock of the builders merchants, Horrocks, was more than usually spectacular.

P.B.

The junction of North Street, West Street and High Street, past which all traffic once crawled, is overlooked by some interesting architectural styles. The solid Georgian property on the left housed the Westminster Bank, while to the right, the mock-Tudor pub is in itself a memorial to a once important Portsmouth brewery, Brickwoods.

P.B.

St Peter's Square and Chapel of Ease built in 1789. It became redundant when St James's Church was built in 1840 and later served as the Town Hall, staged dances and entertainment, then became the Pavilion Cinema in 1912. It was later taken over by a builders merchants who restored the fabric. It is now a café with a pleasant 'Continental' courtyard.

P.B.

Emsworth East c.1970. By the end of the 1960s the town's changing nature is much in evidence. Almost gone are the trades of milling, brewing, ship-building and fishing. The marina, filled with shiny modern yachts, replaces the timber seasoning pond, and houses for a growing population cover several of the former shipyards. The Slipper Mill, albeit converted into flats, still stands at the head of the millpond, and the inner relief road has helped to ease traffic congestion in the town centre.

The Emsworth inner relief road, opened in 1974, sweeps across the top right of the picture. Quay Mill, which still guards the seaward end of the millpond, is now home to Emsworth Slipper Sailing Club which can cause confusion with Slipper Mill on the other millpond. Shipbuilding took place on the eastern shore until the enclosing bank formed the pond c.1760. The white building projecting into the pond was a malt house to a nearby brewery.

C.J.B.

The inner relief road cut through North Street, reducing the grounds of the Victoria Cottage Hospital, seen just above the roundabout. To the right of the hospital is the fire station and old Council Office building which is now home to the Museum of the Emsworth Maritime & Historic Trust. On the right of the picture a complex of sheltered housing covers the site of the old British Legion Club.

C.J.B.